Fort Gorgeous

Fort Gorgeous

Angela Vogel

The National Poetry Review Press
Aptos, California

The National Poetry Review Press
(an imprint of DHP)
Post Office Box 2080, Aptos, California 95001-2080

Fort Gorgeous Copyright © 2011 Angela Vogel

Printed in the United States of America
Published in 2011 by The National Poetry Review
Press

ISBN 978-1-935716-10-5

Cover artwork by Patricia Van Lubeck
"Araucaria velum," 120 x 8o cm oil painting
vanlubeck.com

The National Poetry Review Press
(an imprint of DHP)
Post Office Box 2080, Aptos, California 95001-2080

Fort Gorgeous Copyright © 2011 Angela Vogel

Printed in the United States of America
Published in 2011 by The National Poetry Review
Press

ISBN 978-1-935716-10-5

Cover artwork by Patricia Van Lubeck
"Araucaria velum," 120 x 8o cm oil painting
vanlubeck.com

Fort Gorgeous

Angela Vogel

The National Poetry Review Press
Aptos, California

for L. and M.

TABLE OF CONTENTS

I

II

III

I

LOST COLONY

I'm the gunsmith. You're the third Smith
in a row calculated by planters.

Look through my mosquito glasses
at our island hefted by the seat of its sweet

vine and Oh say what you see. Us winging
hiatus from the Virgin Queen, a cup

of army chowder in exchange for the bling.
She christens Virginia on a Dare, he's

the White guy gone for reinforcements.
Our plans dry up in dribs and drabs.

Some of us get a hatchet job. Others
defortify. The islanders don't think

we're magic anymore, magic meaning
pox-protected creatures packing heat.

Someone's thrown our throne a wrench,
a gag order, chiefly. Directionally lame,

we're unsettling, gypsy, carved with the
anonymity of a Mr. & Mrs. Smith.

POVERTY DRIVE-IN

Yeah, we're in here. Surprised
our love shack's electric? It's not all
clotheslines and mowers, yo.
Not all smack and blow. Who cares
our Beware of Dog lacks teeth.
The broken windows will rattle
you. Speaking of, what did Glenda
the Good Welfare Witch warn
about burning the WIC at both ends?
(Pretty fire! Pretty fire!)
Old dude hosing lawn toys in his robe again
is out there tossing sausage to the ferals.
Never mind the corporate shits
want to occlude his view. The word ghetto
sounding more like get to.
Our free bunnies are plastered on
Joy White posterboard. Our lot's
condemned to the value of squat.
One day here (Holy tot snot!)
is as good as its sequel (Holy milk crate!).
Take a look at what's flowering
under your neighbor's hood—
tattered teens like pistols
waving at you and your happy.

SUBAQUEOUS

Mine, a duck float that was no match
for a claw tub, that was no tub but a river

banked on depositing quick turns of luck,
mummy stuck, watered-down version

of siblings who feel my rib when they swim.
Lifejacketed groom in the murk, cerebral jerk

gone from shallow to sea trench to squirt,
now my cold slur, bottom cur, flotatious

Eddy buoy bejoyed. Me, three sacraments
at once: birth, wed, and dust. Her drowned

applause, unknown cause, moan hushed with
rock. High time she docked like this

submarooned beauty! Come get her sweetpea,
sandflea, stewed-in tsunami. It's motherly

duty to offer some help: sleeper sofa in
coral or kelp? No more ocean

braggadocio or under-represented.
Instead, I'll take the higher ground,

ignore the coy and the hoi polloi.
According to them it's mechanical trouble:

my hand up, her hand-me-down.

MISSING MUM

There is no mother in this paperback. A mother
would make all the hell your protagonist catches
for naught. Instead, there are intervals of knitting
before the veins get ironed out. Maybe a fish wife
after the first gets away. If Dad hits the motherlode,
Bathsheba's been reading the paternal sutra and up
she strides like castrati. As any child of remarriage
can swear on a stack, this is something you carry
all the sandwich-making days of your life. But then,
girls without mothers make excellent wives. They suffer
from motherlust. They see your mother as a Cartesian
egg, its carton dated, rolling near the edge. At times
you'll have to needle through the neighbor's lawn
to find your little Frankenstuff burying her family's shame
spiral. These times a pod of chocolates and a flower
borealis help repopulate her past. Alas, this can't last,
the tale must go on, etc. In the non-Mother Goose version,
the black sheep returns. As you count backwards,
she leaps from the rail.

THE CLAW

Swinger, come hither.
Gird yourself against my steel.
You'll shut my claptrap.
You'll pound my sand.
In me is your chance at Romance's
random number generator turned
verb, as in To Create
your own little-novice-in-truck;
to judge, descend, stick around
& manipulate joy.
If everything loose is a marriage,
everything tight is a wedding
carrying a bouquet of weld.
When the middle roaders come
they'll be light as kites,
the men stood like cranes
to get something olé.
Your escape clause? All fumble
trouble and out-louvered
luck. Mine? An arcane skill
of drag and tip. Love,
I've got the teeth for it.

VENUS FLYTRAP

I opened —bi-stable— the botanist's tale.
Tripped up the tongue on a rosette digest.
The heart was heart-shaped and flat, terminal
lobes hinged midrib. Because I tolerated fire well,
I splayed my sundews. Who among you
understands the muscipula meshwork that takes in
like love? Ol' fused tooth is telegraphing red
sunsets again. Because I sniffed around Vulnerable,
I knew dentates mutate in the carnivorous bowl.
(A plant that eats meat? How newsy! How neat!)
Outside I zipped around quick, like museum bird extinct,
super silliest in the hair-brained schemata. Outside
I dodged a reflexive armada. (See *Mary's violet eyes*
make boys' flies flutter.) I was the freak Darwin
shook from the trees. When the world pimped,
I primped. When the world pinched, I nipped.

THE HUNTSMAN'S RESUMÉ

Oh, I'm ready for the chase. The green pelts,
the headless acorns. In the loom
of an over-improved forest, I'm reminded
that most of the world has moved on
to gathering. For days the slow road
to the lecturing wife, the pound-dog mother.
Even my sword overextended. Yada, yada, yada.
So at word Queenie's bent on a piece
of reflective crap, I leave them home. Shalom.
(Correction: Technically I captured S.W.'s
heart—witness her gratitude.) I'm the hapless
schmuck whose goose is never cooked,
the ten in a 90% chance of moral drizzle.
The boys call me whipped but I don't feel pain
since I failed the art of sensitivity.
Yesterday someone phoned about the Fair Chase
Act: I was reindeer hunting in Greenland.
They're either for me or they're stew,
and if they're stew they can't complain
about this dying anodyne that impressed
the hell out of women once, pre-Bambi effect,
pre-"You're a G.D. paleolith!" upon a time
when acquiring was hip and what you clubbed,
you knew, required goggles formed from beer.

THE ENCHANTED FOREST

As promised we were under a spell.
The Crooked Man, for example, wasn't faking
his complaint. The house was an abomination
in an otherwise orthogonal world,
while the river lay with its blouse undone.
A bit garish considering the place could be seen
squatting dark values from the road,
oystering strange fugues.
Were we harebells or hell's bells? We couldn't tell
a poppy from a polyp if it blew up our noses,
yet we were part of this pile up, this à la carte home
of crumbling lines and rain bloated biscuits.
At the rabbit hole we paused for malted tea
and an off-colored tale of parents who didn't know right
from left, up from down, spinach from kale,
reminders that we never look up without a planetarium
ticket or a beer. Charming really, if Maslow's pyramid
did say so itself. We drank our thimbles
when things grew increasingly incorrect:
We were fungus under a mushroom's nail,
cob from a giant's teeth, a one-size slipper with the toes
lopped off. The cheekbones of cities offered us coffee
and a hundred year warranty on a Beauty-rest.

Our salesman was undoubtedly a prince.
After his pitch, he slid a happy ending
across the uber-modern table.
Someone somewhere pulled some strings:
we knew because a wooden hand arrived
to dot the *must-die*'s, cross *To your good health*.

MEDICINE CHESTS

circa 1960 have a slit for the disposal of razor blades
that looks like a vent for siphoning bad smells:
rubbing alcohol, mercurochrome, and chewable St. Joe's.
But I knew after dad flicked a sharp one down the hole
that double-sided safety razors weren't always safe
unless discarded between the drywall and a beam.
Picture a funeral of half sharp razors rusting in peace,
saving the Our Town babies from sluicing their wrists.
(The guy who played Daddy on Father Knows Best –
Robert Young? help me here—would be toast.)
Hence the advent of coinbank slots in medicine chests,
though you have to wonder what else gets deposited
and if an owner ever drops a note of explanation
down there or some money, thinking he'll be back for it
later like Carl Binkham's dobermans,
left with my folks while he went to run errands.
The story goes that he loaned my dad a thousand dollars
when he came to pick them up, two days before
he got arrested for robbing a Maryland National Bank.
The whole thing is a terrible moral dilemma:
who to pay back, Carl or the bank?
It's a conflict because you're not a bad guy;
you want to fold the bills into tiny origami,

and you wonder how the hell this is happening
to you and why didn't he think to specify
the type of errand and who did he tell
and when are they coming.
Trouble is a snowball on a fast hill,
you're about to find out,
and as every good archeologist worth his weight
in shale will tell you, the harm is in the hiding.
Still, you decide to play it safe,
to do the smart thing,
which is to take this blunt instrument
and lodge it where no one will look for twenty,
maybe thirty years,
since by then there'll be new signers
and co-signers and a good laugh will be had
by all over the advent of the electric shave.

RAGE

"One day I'll become an earthquake if I get any madder."

-Seven-year old girl

Where does it get off dogpiling in the mind
instead of steaming off the top? The rage

had filled up vessels, penned the poison letter
with its episodic wrath. For awhile, it single

filed. Anger was to pan flute as calm was
to code I couldn't break. Those days

the seabed quaked under consequence's
feet, doors slamming: dormant, doormat.

But then it hit me! Rumbles were so '50s!
Their epic center left cracks in the casement.

Their legacy was a hair trigger marriage.
Where was love's escrow to soften the blow?

And where would mad go if the disaster
were natural, the divorce no-fault?

WE'LL GO FOR THE JUGGLER

I tell the next person with an ear for news
about the train passing over Lord Street,
behind the Goodwill, each link brandishing
Ringling Bros. and Barnum & Bailey,
as in the traveling circus,
as in the greatest show on earth and possibly
other planets had the queue gone that far,
two carnies with teeth like constellations
standing on the platform doing the Queen's
wave, wistful and elephantine,
as if a congress of trained animals should maraud.
As if it wasn't bad enough that I was –ta da– late,
now –poof– my job is gone. Now best I board
this town without a zip than go crackers or go ape.
If I'm better than lucky, the strongman will show
me the ropes: We'll walk a fine line
around the cut-up's knife, jump a Hippodrome
of hoops. When I meet the beaut
who's his six o'clock shave, I'll be the schtick-
wreck behind their life between rings
(when really that fire went out swords ago).
We'll headline together the show to end shows:
me, the unwashed, and their pretty Penny.

TATTOO

It's written all over you. Your woad
that might have circled iceman's lips,
or hand-pricked tits in Micronesia. The flaw
of pallor, non-rigor, and your answer:
shot-in-the-arm reinforcements like war
bruises blooming. The way your dermis feathers
paintly. How you're a tablecloth set for the enemy
with too much embroidery, a midriff monarch
hinting felicity. Layers before anesthesia numbed us
to sinks of body ink, you drove us down this indelible
street. The family impound lot of rust and trouble.
The fine line between forever and never-
mind. Our guess? A single jab punctuated by years.
Our fear? Much needling before the pain drew you out.

II

LOVE SONG FOR MANGA

You're the girl I love, the girls I love,
Bishōjo conflated with *Moe*.
I wanna hold your *mangaka-*
drawn hand, go post-apocalyptic
for you. You're the worrisome line on my palm,
the box too small for no.10 mail.
You're a graveyard of catalogues
in manga cafés, the inkspot
where fandom blow moula & *kissa*.
At times you are webmanga,
worldmanga, AmericanGirl manga.
Your *chibi* are alien, techno,
they hold the Lord's roof.
They are *ecchi* and modded,
they are nature's hosanna.
I'm your best shot at reaching
the sky above *yonkoma*,
your ticket bye-bye to *shōjo-ai*,
my moonpie. So what
if we fight? The physics are toon.
Those that need to hang
from cliffs do. Oh sweatdrop
pursed with oodles of yen,

how many flaps with wild Western men
pitching tents? And what then?

TRYST

I'd been sunning all day. Christ,
you can't buy the kind of burn a farmer gets
and yet there I was, trying to impress her,
she of the Many Mice who grained
her tongue into my phone to ask the services
of Morpheus in my stead.
If love takes three times the length it should,
who can blame a man for picking sweet
over salt, bliss over pain?
The body responds like timber
under the tiniest fuse. Nothing to pluck interest
in tad, scant impressions.
Listen for what's not being said
by the sheriff logging the tale.
Some of it's boondoggle and some of it pride,
but the gist is there was a feast
and a fire and somewhere in between heat
that evaporated like a Kansan rain.

SWEET KATE,

But oh, your sprites and vineys! My toothy
pulpit has been cherry brushed. That is to say,
décored. Meaning, we never matched. Meaning
all the botanical garden is divvied up.
Cross polinizing is fertile BS for the birds,
so how can I compare to sinner's pot
in a temperatured terrarium? Every night
they better light you 'til the Ask-Me's form
a congo line of know. Check the pre-schooled hands
that summer in: No one can out-mist them.
Marvel that the boutonnières invest.
Marvel that we safe-house token herbs.
Our plant museum is astroturf: winter interest's
gift to us. What was once upon a bee is now
microbial globe. Weather loved or not.

"NO FAT CHICKS" (popular beach t-shirt)

Imagine what you make of me.
Adipose planets orbit my knees.

My ankles are tabernacles to a goddess
of feed. Saccharin beads on me.

When my body dies, my soul will rise
like the steam from a jelly roll.

It's soluble, what eats me. You,
who do not derive glee from ghee,

could swap vapid for lipid and still
we wouldn't mix (though both victims

of the boardwalk tease). While shore
girls wave from little white tanks,

Joe's EAT AT lights put me at ease.
At twenty-four, your blackbird's baked,

a song of six-packs rising from your pie.
Why am I your poster child

for reductive math, your sacrifice
by sandwich board? Congratulations,

guy, on raising Cain, our diet erudite,
our fop, for whom I'm not pretty

or pleasing with sugar on top.

FROG TSAREVNA

(on an exhibition of Russian folk art)

Three princes, like wishes, shoot an arrow
for a bride. A little like putting a pea
under your mattress, but that's fine,
these are men in a Russian version of Grimm.
The youngest, Tsarevich Ivan, lands a frog
who is, inside, a princess.
We don't see her metamorphosis,
only the beginning of what could be three ends
(that magic number again):
1.   The arrow frees the woman from her
        curséd life with toads.
        (Happy ever after to that.)
2.   The arrow grazes, then angers, her.
        (Symbolism.)
3.   The frog is tragically killed, releasing
        the woman long enough for the prince
        to see what he has won/lost.
        (Introspection, of course.)
The prince's cloak exhales a dragon,
his bow drops in surprise, the sea behind boils
oiled tsunami.
We don't know why, and what's the point?

A happier kingdom?
A missive on the randomness of grief?
Perhaps he should have staked his odds instead
on old-fashioned love, swapped his duds
for peasant garb, trolled the village looking for the one
creature worthy of a crossbow to the heart.

GREEN GODDESS SALAD

After my friend showed me Henry Miller's
Commandments, came publication, fame,
an appearance on Oprah explaining
how my mother taught me to hold *le crayon*.
There was snow like tiny parcels delivered for us
and mothers wrought and overweeping
and Charles Chips and bottled beverages
in flavors like sarsaparilla. We recognized a net
gain of something, L's and O's flourished,
green goddess salad on the menu.
To slow this, I buy bikes for everyone to bop
around town; it's possible to make a grand
gesture as this when you're famous and loved
for saying something no one else thought to
or could. We ride slow like you should
if you live in a town stretched short of five
streets, when we realize there's no place to go
and not enough talent in this whole ship to take us
anywhere but here. This means forfeiting
the chips, the pop, the show, my imaginary pencil
lesson with Mum. I want to disappear
in trajectory, but the sycophants are tailing.
Soon there is nothing left but my salad,

a scam, a charlatan, a pickled herring in red.
Next and after there is no one and nothing
except the guy who says he'd spend his last dollar
to undress a goddess, and would I please marry him.

POEM FOR YOUR WEDDING

In place of a traditional gift. A calla lily
on the night stand sprung from the I-dating life,

out of stroking the what-where-how
into the carpal tunnel of love to see up pops who.

How many times it goes awry, even for
        contortionists
who fail to see the pyrotechnics of carrying

a torch. Of course, we cleave. Come Jubilee,
come Bereft of Time for Me, we pad into

wedlock fuzzy on the combination. Our one day
peep-show is supposed to champagne-up the
        stars,

send Name on its maiden trip to sample love's
buffet. If we're honest, we admit our e-spouse

is selling a mouthful of vowels, or the hitch
comes from a trojan kiss. If we're smart,

we sign up á la carte for the whole enchilada,
move slow into the flowering plot of children,

the family gone nuclear, the kin ship sailed.

HOW TO MAKE PAPER

*The paperwork required to adopt internationally
is known to families as "The Paper Chase".*

Steam the little pulps like fallen rice
from a mei mei's hair, the trees of old China
abuzz and aware of lithographer's
children. Add a curl to your weave
so there's dance in the press
(think a day-bed of ink),
but dry and crisp as May in Fuling
where your husband mistook river laundry
for fish in Yangtze's polluted flutes.
Blanching is good, and sublingual is better.
Dub the mish-mash a "web" and let your head
hold the cob. Stop short of the lob
of the guillotine trim, but if you have the chops,
lick some sugar paper, fish paper, Washi
and wax paper. For security paper,
your hands should be clean.
Mummy papers come to you every which way.
Paper aeroplane tab: Crease a sheet
from the ream and release in jet stream.

THE SPRIG OF ROSEMARY

Based on the Spanish fairy tale

That life is a tiny apology is prettier than true.
Straw & card house, straw and cards, and in the end
pieces unlocked the Unhappy and blew the big wedding.
Always a godmother, never a mum, her aphids
of reproduction smelting on tongues, and seeing
as memory's a tough nut to crack, she took a sprig
in her step and a yawn in her gown and set out
to get back Who'd tolerated some drought.

Now rarer than learning your husband's a beast
is winning him back with almonds conceived
elementally, and petticoats, and unwitting thief,
and while Sun, Moon, and Wind could not do enough
to rinse charm over rust, she did mint her own shrubby
sufficient for hubby to realize he'd married her,
wave scat to the carrion, and collect (re-) the trailer.

Here the story veers to Unkind, the man growing
sick and tired, uninspired, the magic of their song
reaching its limit on the spinet. If all this sounds wrong,
remember there's less fairy in this tale than ordinary,
and the henpecked effect is a dull camisole. The lesson
indeed is to never impede memory with frump
since history's a glaze spread to butter it up.

WHAT NELLY SHOULD HAVE SAID THAT DAY ON THE MOOR

Catherine, you wicked girl, even if you do
pick Linton, you'll end up throwing yourself
from great heights. That gypsy up from
motherless mud has hunkered in your blood,
a weed beneath the sheep feeding curlew, grouse
and plover. Every woman loves an interloper,
but this one swears to take it to the grave.
Two birds picking on a third practically light
the torch for trouble, and your name's shorn
on every moorland spore. Small wonder
the magistrate's no cure and your brother's
bottled out. They'll need to call you Heather
to redeem this harebell scheme: unhealthy
dose of ghost once the bloom is off the groom.

FLOWER BED

I marched the little query to the woods,
plied it unspeakably,
it plopped down fast as nature forms a canopy,
it pulled out *Goblin Market* like a pamphlet from a shoe,
said the elements would damage and ferment us,
I heard its motile feet damp the rusting ground,
quinces and greengages smash like cuttle waves,
I trusted there was this way and only this,
you understand why on the snaky path to knowledge,
a charmer in a mossy glen, cloyed with fruit gnashed
from sisters' necks, she sprang from the velvet nap of it,
and I ahead to the edge, a patchwork of tears
and kneaded breads, a poster for *désastre* and *ruine*,
important parapets to walk,
I dillied to its dally, some of it blistered me,
it was modeling a good bit and craning
so that it came down to what it always does:
what did more, adoration or flogging,
its zeitgeist gone, it struggled to ten-hut, it dribbled
the afterbirth of joy, the look of it sanguine,
abloom in a brotherhood of winks and nods,
I plied it like Narcissus, like a joker
sent to penetrate a club,

sweet maroon sumac skirting us, haloed,

waltzing like sugary fire, somewhere off suffering

& singing in a featherless sleep, a manoeuvre

both manly and over.

FORT GORGEOUS

Grandfathers will call you Miss America
coming down the stair. Grandmothers will claim

your DNA's a gift directly from them.
Perhaps you've even heard that no one has

an ugly child, though the world's electrifyingly
wrong, a rival flag with a .22 star,

a pageant question to the answer
swoon, June, bloom, tomb. The truth is

each of us is fading pearlash bruising
toward an orchard of faded pearlash, and you

have chosen Lovely for your stay.
Up from plain dwellers who light the torch

for trouble, or the bridge that only draws
conclusions. Youth's a temporary liege,

spotty clay we calibrate each day
come bedlam or come ogre.

Lo, I become an alcazar and you the ash
circling beauty's rampart. The city

stops watching our balcony scene.

III

GPS: A FAIRYTALE

Out of fire's red flower, what bloomed
was technology.
Through hem and door. Apostolate to blind days
and slow rotations. Epistle to flash and song,
to lucky star populated with crabs and men.
After: obsequious bathers, spray of charm,
grapple of cats mewing.
The math teacher who claimed calculus
was in the trees, correct and grinning.
Nebula of vanished fruit
bloomed like birds. *Wise up!* said with a pound
of fist flourish. All of this suppositional and thin,
a macramé of moths. The whole asynchronous
tundra dropped squarely in our laps.
None of this remotely true.
As you can see, I'm driving home a point
in my Suburban, in my Legend.
A calculated risk, a satellite, and a minister of
logic walk into a bar. Consider this a thumb
map, a pocket allegory to solve for *y* man is king
of man. Not so much a riddle
as a long begotten story, with a protagonist who
once rescued, does not live happily or live forever,
come to think of it after.

ORIGINAL MAN

Likely he was thought an ogre, blinking
and misunderstood for moving to the woods,
but a suggestion like this was the wifely
thing to do, our visits taken in his parlor
of Vermont flame, fall house for this ombudding
festoon. By noon he'd shoot petals from hips
that died gorgeously Georgian, little senators
dropped to earth's floor and raked across
the coals of our tired olfactories. Mistakes
honeysuckled clear to the forest town's edge.
Because I didn't fear him, I let him sing
a song of six-packs, pockets full of sky.
Two up from ash plucked like trumpets
to broaden God's joy, to beatify the spinach
laced trees we didn't know exactly how
sweet. Our home built on outskirts to keep
the wild out. To lure out the wild. The dark
growing darkest when no eyes are upon it.
Our guards hung in mist the way flowers
fell and notch in a long sweating rain.
The way someone with fruit made its blood
ours, first as a dove and later a hawk.
Hawk in the sense of a warring mangrove—

such a sad entity you want to unhand it but can't,
even when you and the man turn afraid and run,
all your fruit bloomed in naked duplicity.

NIGERIAN PHISHING SCAM

From a country she can't map mentally
but recognizes as poor, comes the electronic plea

from Delegate Okonuki whose funds are stuck
in Nigerian money jail. He's official

& it's urgent & not every day
she gets a request out of the big blue skype

to send a deposed king one tenth her
western nest. By virtue of some faith

(his trapped sum being greater than her part),
this instant pirate wants a wire and her

to walk it. His claim is laid over
seas that net good deals in the grand scheme,

or so she feels and so she falls
for this guy's plight, bit by byte. She doesn't see

the pretext in his lettered head, believing
instead a civil servant's sworn reward.

It's not until the social worm hits heart
she feels her chest emptied by his virtual spear,

so convivial his angling for her trust.

MOSQUITO

No skeet shoot. No bag of loot. No red car at the mohito
      bar.
No tropical, smoothie, dusk-breeding floozy. Not
      Deetnik.
Not small fry, bullseye, swarmy *numb-you-at-the-clinic*
      guy.
Not a spit tune. Nor *á la lune.* Nor Penny Dreadful
      dashing goon.
No one's sucker punch. Or liquid lunch. Or mobile unit
      swat team.
No third class anti-histamine. Not public nuisance no. 2,
      Betelgeuse,
or squish & *ewww.* I refuse to be your buzz kill. Or Bill
      Kill. Stop with
job hopper. I prefer pest defense against the stagnant
      waters of my time.
Flavivirus Incubatous, hold the lyme. More like needle-
      nosed plier. Carbon
footprint frequent flier. No-show in repellant court.
      A carapace
whose days are short. Your citronella-fella, posse, Don.
      West of the Nile,
I'm Poké-mon. Health threat on the baby net.
      Never-let'em-see-you-sweat.

FLAME

Scram (which gave us the pig Latin *amscray*)
is traced to underworld and circus slang,
so it's no surprise I associate one with the other,
both a sort of oddball, marivaudage
of sentiment and veil.
Today, after teaching Dante's Inferno
for the umpteenth time,
I brush arms with a beautiful undergrad,
a scrambling by the stairs.
What would Elizabeth Bishop say
to a professor's low crush,
her sufferings in the classroom less of a diversion
than the sexiness of youth learning?
Every term's a metaphor for a carbon-leaf day,
the planets braising slow as spinning tops at rest.
Tonight, I'll walk the dog along our usual path,
pass the 7-11 old and chaffed and red,
wait for the rain to blanche like tadpoles
down a mildewed, fiery lake.

ASPHODEL

"Hearts starve as well as bodies; give us bread, but give us roses."

-James Oppenheim

Hi, I'm Asphodel, the flower of Hell,

King's spear on the Hades plain,

Queen of putting a good face on things,

your southern forget-me-not for this leg

replete with bruised root and foot rot.

(Yes, Virginia, there is a Devil and

he has a green thumb.) Those of you vested

in carnations are free to come (versus

the varieties "at last" or "to go").

Why-Me's take note: I'm a wicked cut.

Bad seed clichés burn me up. I thrive

on full light in my crisis garden parish.

And this backpeddling (to what?)

spells a whole host of trouble. Nothing

strange, just *fleur-de-lis* doused in Miracle

Grow and the occasional weed for greedy

Greek eats. We're the infidels

in an orthodoxy house, the welcome

committee for this shitty city.

When the dead beat their horses (and they do)

for refusing to chew, it's *good grief!*

and *leaving so soon?* You'll have to sue

if you want the thieving rose instead,

that social-climbing perennial enemy.
We've blood enough on our hands
without fielding those pricks.

AMERICAN REPRESENTATION

The idea was to rotate them
like 19th century dancers doing the do-
si-do, a polite curtsy as close as you got
to being in bed with your interests,
fluid as the Virginia Reel and nearly
as simple, novices welcome, a party
man taking your hat at the door,
variance frowned, the penultimate social
mother, sister, uncle waving your card
on oakey floor, sworn to honor
a partner and corner, judiciously tapping
the social cadence, a cache of ugly beaus
your only job for the day.

ROSEBUD, OR NOW THAT I AM OLDER

Another day, another bother, I need to pull
the rosebush next to this old house easement.
Too many days have passed in shade and brown
petals poised like questions on the portico.
I've avoided the prick and hook of thumb
so long I barely notice a new year or sky
claim the space above my court.
Here's a set of London-dark days
like mops arranged by handle size.
Here's a hot rag stinging with vermouth
to ward off the untoward.
I'm nothing special that a thought as simple
as the river couldn't wipe away,
even sticks in an evenfloe inherit the shape
of the bathysphere.
This is something humans have to practice.
Watch nine monks set up a mandala
only to blow it away; this will worm the fleeting
nature of restraint into your ear.
See a mash of perennials in the soil around
our dearth, lauded when the sun turns them
neckward in the pot. Push your hands far down
the dirt, feel it grip your insubstantial grasp,
make you mindful this too shall last.

JUBILEE YEAR

The only thing left is to hang
our hat on regret's haberdasherie.
Once we're cured of lucky:
little-sisters-of-the-mall get curbed.
Balanced budgets everywhere
get talked down from the ledge.
The good-graced among us
pass the sugar bowl of debt.
If I could bank on what it takes
to pep us into rally, I'd dub myself
loss leader. I'd ide for a time
the sirs of overspent kept
the mistresses of thrift,
lording forgiveness over them.

TISSOT'S *WAITING FOR THE FERRY*

These are gentlepeople waiting
outside Dreary Station, the weight
of the industrialized world upon the mother,
who's a coon wrap sagging on an iron bench.
She's young, but something's zapped her.
The boy slogs "junior banker," listening to Pa
regale the tale of the Merchant Marine,
but it's the hat and glove girl
who brims excitement for the fleet,
skimming the rails, smokestacks
gathering doom in the space above her head
so that she nearly strays the canvas looking out.
Who guessed so many shades of gray
could convene upon a pier? The only light
Tissot can spare seeps around the girl like yeast,
rickets all that hold her back from a harbor/soot
au pair. The threat is that she'll slip away
from this civility, become the poster gal
for the KABOOM! factory,
our millinery a pulsing starboard
on a dim sum shore.

THE HERMITAGE

"Private: Please Bypass"

Say you come to your own snowy Frost fork.
Say the man on the plane was no Verdi opera,
but pumped up like yeast with a somnambulist twist.
Meaning, in your book, a lot of pulp and circumstance,
flak and flutter. Imagine the garden outpulsing
what only a loon could dispatch, that you open
the doors and there are the people. To the left
of the throngs is vintage decay, to the right
the sheerness of sheep. No one has asked you to decide
or cut ties or take up a wish. God is a reveler in smites,
you are sure, just as you knew the wild goose
was for you, and the blue point of view, and layer six
where the Seven-Bean dips. At fortitude's entrance
a note names you King, which pleases you plainly.
Tho' far be it from dwelling. Where a recluse is
not wrecked and not loose, that'd be hell.

SANITARIUM

They all end in fire.

Twenty pivots after the bore d'oeuvres
and flatter-me-chatter, I'm cast as daft.
Boo that! I've the brain of a dipsomaniac,
the stain of disdain. If the pilot is out,
I can't take the blame. Grim and grimmer,
a primer for the plank. I drank the stew,
I bought the farm, I plucked the rubaiyat
by its arm. Fire up the fruit flies
while we woman-up the yard.
Our nutty bash has come unhinged:
we dish, we dash, we swoon, we yarn.
We lo' disease, we burn the barn.

RIP VAN WINKLE,

Check out your gnomes. They are the paprika
of landscape, garden variety boys
in distressed salut. They don't give a rip
about your old lady's manor. They are squatters,
mooching. Twenty years of deep sleep.
They peel at the post like paint dressed in rust.
If you must choose decay, note the difference
at least in *overlook* and *look over*.
All the sons in your image are taking
a stand, dirt nap admiring, ornamentally wived.
There were extra yards they might have gone,
but at working stiff stature, their lamps petered out.
May they awake in laborious times.
May they keep an idle foot in the fire.
You have all overslept. You're welcome.

HISTORY TV

The telly's back-peddling documentary
in pacific time, and plying me to *Armchair west!*
with its Michigan heroine, its shandrydan.
All hail the lime worm sailed around on thistle!
All hail the crackerjack and his paper riddle!
The neckerchief alone is worth a kernel
of surprise, though it's all been done before,
fountains dripping news the Romans sent
on loan, Manifest Destiny around the world
to the left. Even greed's foretold:
the man who can't hold water constructs
an aqueduct and the band hums
bars of gold. The galaxy's his luxury;
history's his graffiti. His gaffe is thinking
Desert could be outfitted completely. Nothing
left to pan for, can-can, or speak easy. Nothing
but to channel how his town lived briefly.

ACKNOWLEDGMENTS

My thanks to the editors of the following publications in which these poems or earlier versions of them first appeared:

The American Poetry Journal: "Asphodel"

Barn Owl Review: "The Claw"

Border Crossing: "What Nelly Should Have Said That Day on the Moor"

Cave Wall: "No Fat Chicks"

Cimarron Review: "Poverty Drive-In"

Drexel Online Journal: "Frog Tsarevna"

Folio: "Tissot's *Waiting for the Ferry*"

Good Foot: "Flame"

Gulf Coast: "Venus Flytrap"

The Journal: "The Hermitage"

MiPOesia: "Tryst"

The National Poetry Review: "Flower Bed," "History TV," "Lost Colony," "Rip Van Winkle," "Sanitarium," "The Sprig of Rosemary," and "Subaqueous"

Pebble Lake Review: "Medicine Chests"

POOL: "Green Goddess Salad"

Potomac Review: "American Representation"

roger: "Poem for Your Wedding" and "We'll Go for the Juggler"

The Southeast Review: "The Enchanted Forest," "GPS: A Fairytale," and "The Huntsman's Resumé"

Sou'wester: "Fort Gorgeous" and "Mosquito"

The Valparaiso Review: "Rosebud, or Now That I Am Older"

"Ashodel," "The Claw," and "The Huntsman's Resumé" were reprinted on *Verse Daily* (www.versedaily.org).

"GPS: A Fairytale" won *The Southeast Review* Poetry Prize, 2008.

"Love Song for Manga" appeared in *Best New Poets 2008*.

"Rosebud, or Now That I am Older" was published in the chapbook *Social Smile* (Finishing Line Press, 2004).

Several of these poems were completed with support from the Maryland State Arts Council and the Mary Anderson Center for the Arts.

Thanks to C.J. Sage for believing in my work and working tirelessly to present it in book form.

Thanks to my friends Sally Rosen Kindred, Bernadette Geyer, Renee Soto, Marcus Myers, Julie Brooks Barbour, Luke Johnson, Mary Biddinger, and Sandra Beasley for their close readings, generous support, and cheerleading at every post.

Most of all, thanks and love to my family for lifting me up and creating an environment conducive to imagination and growth.

Also from The National Poetry Review Press:

Lucktown by Bryan Penberthy

Bill's Formal Complaint by Dan Kaplan

Gilgamesh at the Bellagio by Karl Elder

Legend of the Recent Past by James Haug

Urchin to Follow by Dorine Jennette

The Kissing Party by Sarah E. Barber

Deepening Groove by Ravi Shankar

The City from Nome by James Grinwis

Loud Dreaming in a Quiet Room by Betsy Wheeler

Please visit our website for more information:

www.nationalpoetryreview.com